Contents

Introduction ... 2

Unit 1 Settings ... 8
Writing focus: note-making; turning notes into complete sentences; writing story settings; improving story openings.

Unit 2 Plays ... 14
Writing focus: writing dialogue; writing the opening, middle and final scenes of a playscript.

Unit 3 Non-chronological reports ... 20
Writing focus: labelling; note-making; tuning notes into complete sentences; planning, writing and editing a non-chronological report.

Unit 4 Fables ... 26
Writing focus: writing stages of a known fable as a storyboard; writing a storyboard plan for an alternative version; writing an alternative version.

Unit 5 Performance poetry ... 32
Writing focus: writing descriptive sentences; drafting and polishing a senses poem; writing a chorus.

Unit 6 Instructions ... 38
Writing focus: writing notes and lists; turning notes into instructions; revising and editing instructions.

Unit 7 Extended stories ... 44
Writing focus: writing notes and lists; writing a storyboard plan; writing the opening, 'problem' and ending of an adventure story.

Unit 8 Humorous poetry ... 50
Writing focus: writing an alliterative alphabet poem; writing tongue twisters; writing rhyming couplets; writing and polishing a nonsense poem.

Unit 9 Recounts ... 56
Writing focus: writing notes and lists; writing a letter or e-mail; writing a newspaper report; improving a recount.

Word classes ... 62

Glossary ... 64

Index ... inside back cover

Introduction

Welcome to *Writers' World*

This *Handbook* is a guide to help you become a better writer. It helps you through the stages of the writing process, giving tips and advice along the way to help you improve your writing.

How to use this Handbook

Sometimes your teacher will ask you to read a section and perhaps write with a friend or do a *Try this!* activity.

Other times you might be asked to do a *Quick write* activity, this is exactly what the name says – you will do a very quick writing activity.

Sometimes you will see *Challenge* activities. You can do these if you finish your work early or if you have some spare time.

The writing process

Thinking and Planning → Drafting → Revising

1 Thinking and planning
- Use planning frames and storyboards.
- Think about:
  what you are going to write, who will read it, how it will be organised.
- Write notes – not full sentences.

2 Drafting
- Follow your plan.
- Turn your notes into a rough version of the finished piece.
- Try different ways of saying things.

3 Revising (see page 4)
- Check your writing makes sense.
- Make changes and cross out parts that you are not happy with.

There are some parts of the book that help you use it and help you understand what you are reading.

Word classes   If you want to know more about words and the jobs they do in a sentence, use the *Word classes* chart (pages 62–63).

Glossary   If you aren't sure what certain words mean, this is the place to look (page 64).

Index   If you need help with parts of your writing, use the *Index* to look things up (see inside back cover).

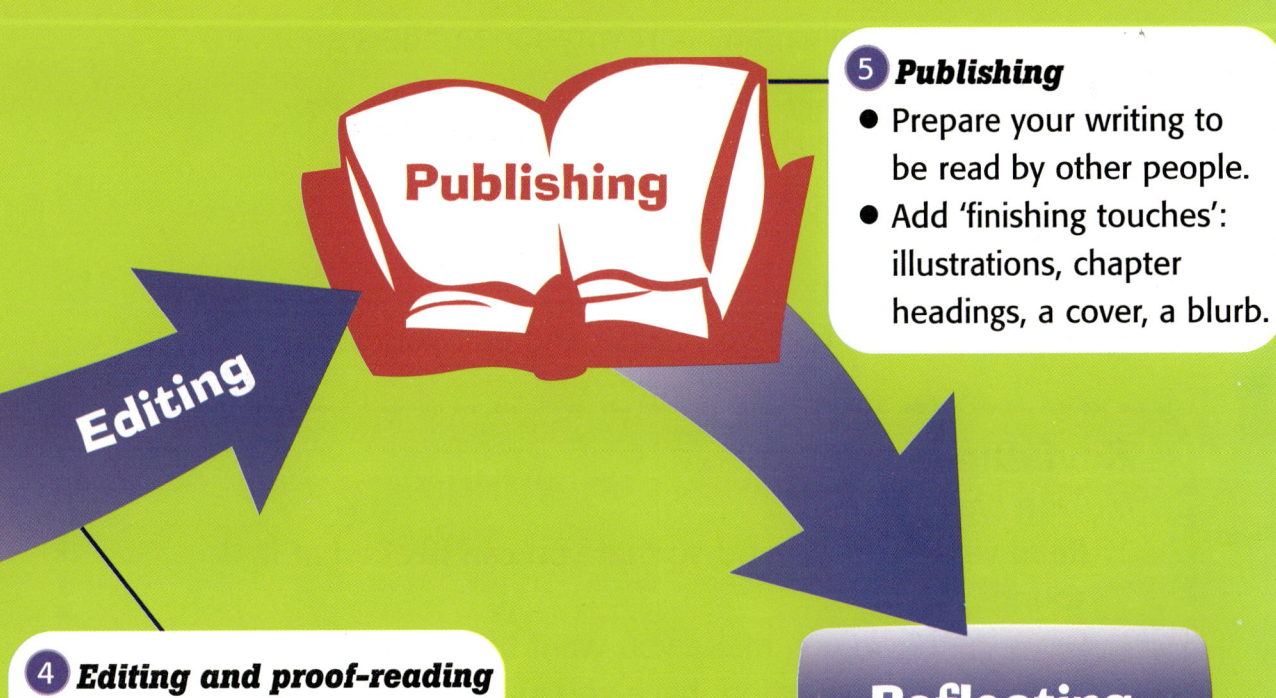

Publishing

5 *Publishing*
- Prepare your writing to be read by other people.
- Add 'finishing touches': illustrations, chapter headings, a cover, a blurb.

Editing

4 *Editing and proof-reading (see page 5)*
- Check spelling, grammar and punctuation.
- Look at the order of words in sentences. Could you make your sentences more interesting by changing the word order?

Reflecting

6 *Reflecting*
- Read your published writing.
- Which parts are you pleased with?
- Think about future ideas for writing.

A critical friend

Writers often ask friends to read their work and to tell them what they think about it. Friends can help you by:

- talking about parts of your writing they think are good
- asking questions about parts they don't quite understand
- talking about the way you have organised your writing and the words you have chosen.

A guide to being a critical friend
Some ideas to help you:

- find a part that you like and tell your friend why
- ask your friend to explain any part you don't understand
- give ideas for words that would make the writing more interesting.

Writing checklists

Use these checklists to help you revise and edit your writing.

Revising checklist
Making big changes.

1. Read your writing aloud so that you can hear what it sounds like.
2. Does the beginning make you want to keep reading?
3. If you are writing fiction, have you given the reader an idea of the setting?
4. Have you given the reader an idea of what the characters are like by describing what they look like, the way they speak and how they behave?
5. Is the ending good or do the characters go home for tea or wake up and find it was all a dream?
6. If you are writing non-fiction, is it clearly organised?
7. Are the facts accurate?

Editing checklist
Making small changes.
1. Read your writing to look at how you have used words.
2. Would changing the order of words in a sentence help?
3. Have you used a variety of verbs, adverbs and adjectives to make your writing interesting?
4. Can you take out any nouns and use pronouns instead?
5. Are there words you have used a lot? Can you change any of them? You could use a thesaurus to help you.
6. Think about how the characters are feeling. It helps to write a description about how they behave.
7. In non-fiction, do you need to add features like diagrams, labels or captions?
8. Have you used any technical language you need?

Proof-reading
This means checking spelling and punctuation to see whether you could improve your writing any more. There are special marks that editors use to show the changes they want to make. Here are some you could use when you proof-read writing:

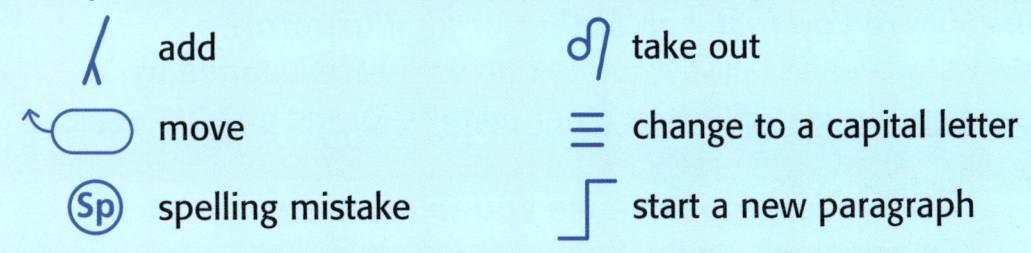

⋏	add	♂	take out
⌒	move	≡	change to a capital letter
(Sp)	spelling mistake	⌐	start a new paragraph

This is how you use them:

What's for tea?

Mum, dad and I went camping at the seaside for our summer holiday ~~this summer~~. We packed our tent, lots of food and a new gas stove. (We had to take a lot of equipment.) It was hot when we got there, so Mum and I went for a swim while Dad put up the tent. After swimming I was *really* hungry. But when we tried to cook tea, the gas stove didn't work!

Enjoy your writing and remember – write every day!

Meet an author

COLIN McNAUGHTON

Colin McNaughton is one of the UK's most popular authors. Colin writes and illustrates children's books and humorous poetry. He has produced over ninety books and has won many awards for his work. Read the interview and find out more about him.

Q: *Which do you prefer, writing or illustrating?*
A: I like the excitement of coming up with a good idea – in words and quick sketches – but I also enjoy getting the picture as right as I want it to be.

Q: *Why do you do both jobs?*
A: Because I enjoy doing both and because the words and the pictures come together in my head as an idea.

Q: *Which were you first – an author or an illustrator?*
A: I always drew and I always wrote but work wise I started by illustrating stories written by other authors for the first 2-3 years.

Q: *How long does it take you to illustrate a book?*
A: It depends on the book – some take a few months, some take a few weeks, some take years.

Q: *Where did you get the idea for Preston Pig from?*
A: Probably from a book I wrote and illustrated years ago called 'Fat Pig'. The pig was not called Preston then but he wore white dungarees with pink stripes.

Q: *Do you always write funny poetry? Why don't you write serious poetry for adults?*
A: I do. Lots of my poems are funny but there are a few quieter ones in my books. All are serious even if they sound funny. I write for the child in all of us, so that means adults too.

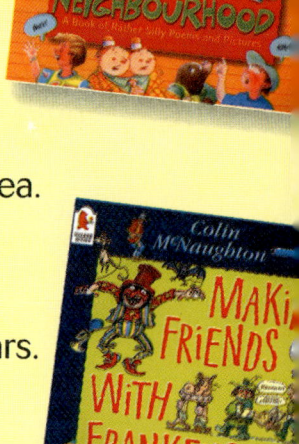

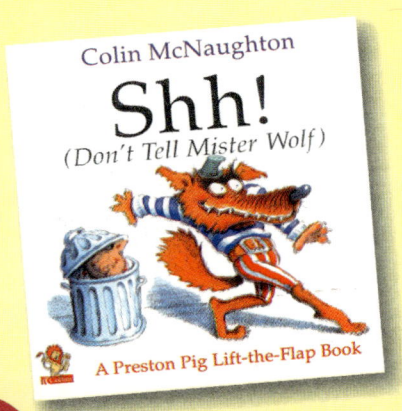

Q: *Where do you get your ideas for funny illustrations?*
A: All around me.

> **Q:** *Who is your favourite character from your books?*
> **A:** I like all my characters but perhaps I do like Preston a bit more than the others.

Q: *Are the people in your books real people you know?*
A: Of course they are.

> **Q:** *Which do you do first, the pictures or the words, when you write your books?*
> **A:** Both at the same time. The minute I think of an idea I can see the drawing in my head.

Q: *What is your favourite poem that you have written?*
A: 'I feel sick' from 'Wish You Were Here (And I Wasn't)' because when I read it in public I can pretend to be sick, which is much nicer than being sick in real life. I also like 'Cockroach Sandwich' from 'Making Friends with Frankenstein':

> Cockroach sandwich
> For my lunch,
> Hate the taste
> But love the crunch!

Q: *Who is your favourite author and why?*
A: R. L. Stevenson who wrote 'Treasure Island', because the book has got everything I like.

Q: *Can you give me any tips about illustrating?*
A: Just keep drawing, drawing, drawing…

> **Q:** *What advice would you give to someone who wanted to be a writer?*
> **A:** Just keep writing, writing, writing… and reading, reading, reading….

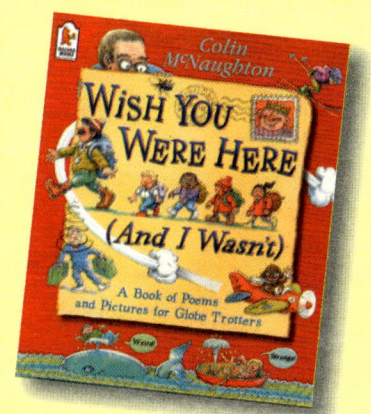

Q: *What do you like doing when you're not making books?*
A: At the moment I enjoy making models of my characters. I've already done Preston, Mister Wolf and Jolly Roger and I'm now working on Captain Abdul.

Unit 1
Settings

Look closely at the illustrations. What can you see?

9

Planning a setting

Setting the scene – Show or tell?
Illustrations in storybooks *show* readers where and when a story is set. When writers write stories without pictures, they have to *tell* their readers about the setting.

Where?
At the beginning of a story, readers need to know where the story takes place. Writers help readers picture the setting by mentioning things that set the scene. So 'blocks of flats' and 'busy pavements' would help a reader think of a town or city scene.

> **Quick write**
> *Write two or three words to describe an underground scene.*

Sentences, sentences, sentences
A writer needs to be sure about how sentences work. A sentence is . . .

- a words of group that sense make
- a sense group that words make of
- a group of words that make sense.

Punctuation box

Try this!

Help a writer to sort out this jumbled advice.

> with a full sentence A starts capital letter with ends and a stop.

Telling the time in stories

When we read the opening lines of a story, we find details about when the story is set.

'*Once upon a time*' usually means long ago.

If we read '*A year ago, when everybody wore rollerblades*' it's clear that the story is not set in the distant past.

Writers give these details early in stories so that readers can imagine the setting for themselves.

Try this!

Read these story openings. When and where do you think they are set? What helped you decide?

1. Long ago, when dragons roamed the world and travelling anywhere was a dangerous adventure . . .
2. All was quiet at number 10 Millennium Street. The snow had muffled the usual rumble of traffic.

Writing a setting

Adding details to the scene
Sometimes writers help readers make pictures in their heads by adding other details to a setting.

Try this!
Read these two passages then discuss them with a friend. Think about:
- what is the same
- what is different
- what each passage tells you.

1. It was a cold and stormy night, clouds covered the moon. The wind blew sheets of rain across the empty street. Not the sort of night to be out.

2. It was a dark night. The street was empty. It was wet and cold. Not the sort of night to be out.

Synonyms
Synonyms are words that have the same or similar meanings. Writers use synonyms to:
- add interesting details
- stop their writing being boring
- keep their readers interested.

Challenge
How many synonyms can you list for the word 'little'?

enormous?
huge?
large?
mighty?

The big waves rolled onto the shore.

Improving writing

Writers need to make sure that their writing makes sense and is interesting for the reader.
These are some of the things writers think about.

1. Does the order need changing?
2. Do any words need changing or taking out?
3. Have words been repeated too much?
4. Is there enough detail?

Five finger check

When you write a setting, ask yourself:

1. How do I make the place clear?
2. How do I make the time clear?
3. Can I improve my sentences?
4. Can I add more detail?
5. Does it make the reader want to read on?

Reflecting and reviewing

What have you learned about writing settings? Swap your setting with a partner. Read it and think about the following points.
1. Can you tell when and where the story is taking place?
2. How have their word choices helped you?

Now complete your review sheet.

Unit 2
Plays

Look closely at the illustration. What is going on?

15

Planning a playscript

What is a play?
Plays are like living stories – the stories are acted for people to see and hear. When we *watch* a play

we can see:
- what the characters do
- how the characters move
- what the characters look like.

we can hear:
- what the characters say
- how the characters speak.

The scenery in the background in plays shows us the setting. When we *read* a story, we have to *imagine* all these things.

Playlet
Read what happened when Jack from the story of Jack and the Beanstalk met Prince Charming.

Jack: Hello! You look as though you need help.
Prince C: I do. I need to get this shoe repaired.
Jack: Hmmm! That's funny, a glass shoe. Don't suppose it's much use. Not like these trainers.
Prince C: That's what I say to my wife. But she will keep on wearing these glass things.
Jack: Take my advice. Tell her it costs too much to repair them. Get her a pair of trainers like these!
Prince C: What's so special about trainers?
Jack: They help you run really fast. And you never know when you might need to do that. Running fast can be very useful.

Speaking

In *stories*, speech marks:
- show when a character speaks
- show what a character says
- separate speech from the rest of the story.

In *plays*, speech marks are not needed because:
- each character is named before they speak
- the words a character says follow their name.

Try this!
Read these two passages.
1. Which is the play?
2. Which is the story?
3. What is the same?
4. What is different?

A

As he ran towards the goal, James slipped in the mud.

'Oh my goodness!' he gasped.

'What's that shining in the grass?' whispered Sam.

B

Narrator:	Two boys, James and Sam, are playing football in the park. James slips in the mud.
James (gasping):	Oh my goodness!
Sam (whispering):	What's that shining in the grass?

Writing a playscript

The role of the narrator
Just like a story, a play has:
- an opening
- a setting
- characters
- something that happens
- an ending

When we write plays, we need to think about how to tell the story to the audience.

In stories, *writers* tell readers about settings and the things characters do.

In plays, a *narrator* can tell the audience these things. The narrator is like a football commentator who tells us what is happening on the pitch.

How to speak
In plays, writers sometimes use verbs to tell actors how to speak. They might want them to shout, whisper or cry. This helps the actors show the audience more about the story and the characters.

These speech verbs are written straight after the character's name like this:

Sam (whispering):		What shall we do?
James (gulping):		I don't know!

Try this!
Speech verbs in plays are written in the present tense. Can you turn these past tense speech verbs into the present tense? For example, 'snarled' becomes 'snarling'.

snarled   muttered   cried   giggled

Challenge
Can you think of a speech verb that is not used in plays?

Five finger check
When you are writing a play, ask yourself:

1. Have I set the scene?
2. What do I want the narrator to say?
3. Have I given my characters names?
4. Have I told them what to say?
5. Have I used speech verbs?

Reflecting and reviewing

What have you learned about writing plays? Talk to a friend. Think about the plays you have just watched.
- Which did you enjoy? Why?

Now complete your review sheet.

Unit 3
Reports

Title — Rabbits

Definition — Rabbits are small (mammals) and can be kept as pets. — technical vocabulary

What they look like — Rabbits weigh between 1kg and 5kg. They (have) long back legs and short front legs. Some rabbits have ears that stand up. Others have floppy ears – they are called lop-eared rabbits. Rabbits' fur (is) short. Their coats can be patterned, speckled or all one colour. Rabbits have sharp front teeth which they (use) for gnawing. — present tense

Lop-eared rabbit

What they eat — Rabbits are herbivores. This means that they do not eat meat. They eat grass and plants like dandelions and chickweed. Pet rabbits will eat dried hay and rabbit food. They also eat most fruit and vegetables. Rabbits need plenty of fresh, clean water.

technical vocabulary
written in 3rd person

Rabbit food

Where they live — Rabbits are very active animals so they need a lot of space. Pet rabbits are kept in hutches with an exercise area and a sleeping area. The hutch should be kept out of the wind and rain. In the summer rabbits can be kept in runs outside.

technical vocabulary

Rounding-off sentence — Rabbits can live for between 6 and 8 years.

Rabbit hutch

- sleeping area
- water bottle
- exercise area

21

Planning a report

What is a non-chronological report?
Non-chronological reports give a reader information about a subject, for example, rabbits. Reports:
- have an introductory statement
- are organised in paragraphs
- are written in the present tense
- sometimes contain labelled diagrams and photographs
- have a closing or rounding-off sentence.

Making notes
When you plan a piece of writing you don't need to write in sentences. You can just write key words and phrases. These will remind you of what you want to write later.

It is useful to group key words and phrases under headings. This keeps your information organised – it won't wander off and get lost. The information under each heading can be used later to organise your writing into paragraphs.

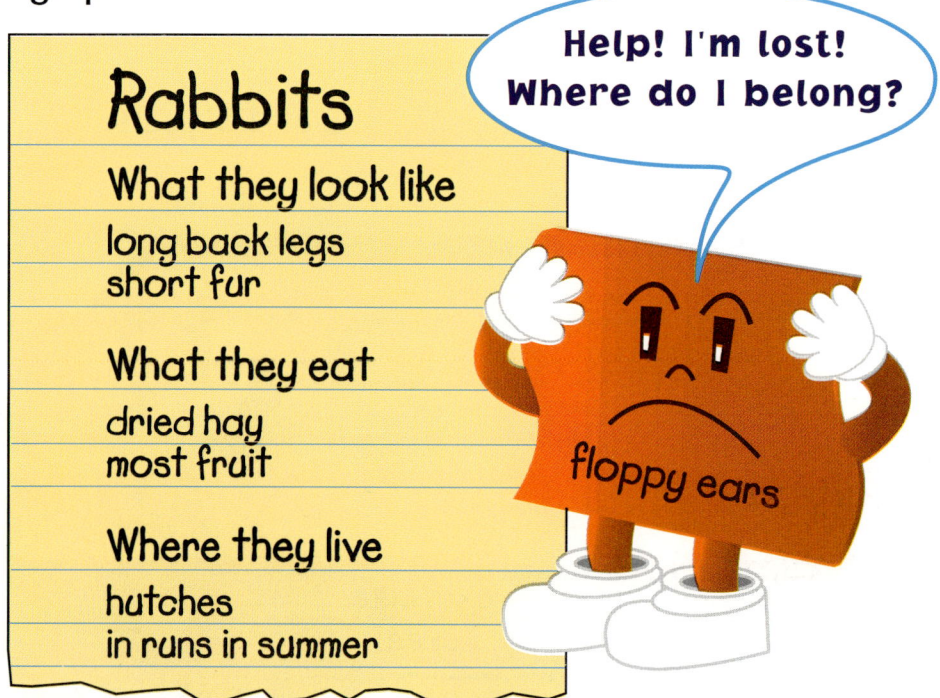

Rabbits

What they look like
- long back legs
- short fur

What they eat
- dried hay
- most fruit

Where they live
- hutches
- in runs in summer

Help! I'm lost! Where do I belong?

floppy ears

Try this!

This writer tried to make notes, but wrote in complete sentences, rather than key words and phrases. Work with a friend. Can you rewrite the sentences as notes?

Camels have one or two humps, depending on what sort they are. There are two sorts of camels. They are called Arabian camels and Bactrian camels. Arabian camels have one hump. Bactrian camels have two humps. Camels can survive for a long time without food or drink because they can live on the fat in their humps.

Challenge
Can you show the information about camels as a diagram?

Writing a report

What is a sentence?

Words have to work hard at becoming a sentence. There are a few rules. Sentences always:

- start with a capital letter
- contain a verb
- contain a noun or a pronoun
- make sense
- end with a full stop, question mark or exclamation mark.

Sometimes writers choose to break these rules.

Try this!

With a friend, look at these. Check them against the list above. Are they sentences?

1. Penguins eat fish.
2. Do penguins eat fish?
3. Penguins
4. Penguins love fish!
5. Penguins fish for fish.

Challenge

Is this a sentence? Why? / Why not?
Fish fish fish.

Verbs

Sentences need verbs. Verbs tell a reader *what* happens in a sentence. For example:
Elephants eat fruit.
They also show *when* something happens.
Rabbits live in burrows. (present tense)
Dinosaurs roamed the earth. (past tense)

Try this!
Look for the past tense verbs in these sentences. With a friend, change them into the present tense.

1. The Silver Wonder ice-cream tasted super.
2. Our local zoo had three unicorns and a woolly mammoth.
3. The computer screen flashed and the adventure began.
4. The strange sea monster caught a cold.

Five finger check

When you are writing reports remember to:

1. Plan the report using notes.
2. Organise the facts into paragraphs.
3. Include an introduction and a closing or rounding-off sentence.
4. Write in the present tense.
5. Include a labelled diagram if necessary.

Reflecting and reviewing

What have you learned about writing reports? Swap your report with another pair. Think about the following points.

1. How is the information organised?
2. Is it written in the present tense?
3. Are there any suggestions you would like to make to the writers?

Now look through your report and complete your review sheet.

Unit 4
Fables

The Boy Who Cried Flood!

A boy was sent to run a bath ready for his little brother. He was fed up because he had to do this every day. He decided to play a trick on his mother. 'Flood! Flood!' he shouted at the top of his voice. 'There's a flood in the bathroom!' Up the stairs raced his mum, leaving whatever she was doing downstairs. When she got to the bathroom and saw that there was no flood, the boy laughed and laughed.

The next day, the same thing happened. 'Flood! Flood!' shouted the boy. When his mother rushed up the stairs and again found that there was no flood, the boy laughed more than ever.

On the third day, the taps got stuck and a flood really did happen. 'Flood! Flood!' shouted the boy. 'Mum, come quickly!' But this time, his mother took no notice. The boy stared sadly at all his little brother's ruined toys floating around the bathroom.

Planning a fable

What is a fable?
A fable is a short story with a special purpose – to help us think about how to behave. For example:
- to tell the truth
- to help other people
- not to be greedy.

The first fables were told and not written down. Storytellers used fables to help people understand the difference between right and wrong.

Fables are usually about animals who act like humans. By the end of the fable the main character has learned a lesson and is left with something to think about.

The thinking point of a fable is called *the moral*. Sometimes the last line of a fable says *'The moral of this story is …'*. Sometimes we need to work out the moral for ourselves.

How did the tortoise beat me?

Story planning
A useful way to plan a story is to use a storyboard. Storyboards can help us to:
- plan in order
- draw main events
- make notes about main events.

The pattern of three

Many stories have a 'pattern of three' in them. These might be:
- three characters, e.g. three Billy Goats Gruff.
- three things, e.g. three wishes
- three events, e.g. Jack's three trips up the beanstalk.

Storytellers use the pattern of three to:
- help listeners or readers to follow the story
- build up excitement
- help readers remember the story.

Challenge
Think of three nursery rhymes or fairy tales that use the pattern of three. List them.

Writing a fable

Adjective advice
Adjectives tell us more about nouns. Writers use them to help readers build up pictures of people, places or things. But beware… too many adjectives can muddle the picture!

Try this!
Read these two sentences. Talk to a friend. What are the differences between the sentences? How did you feel after you had read them?

1. The lost, bewildered, frightened, little boy looked up at the shiny, glittering, sparkling stars and made a special, secret wish.
2. The frightened boy looked up at the glittering stars and made a wish.

Who is telling the story?
Two ways of telling stories are:
- as a character in the story
- as a watcher of the story.

Think about the story of *Jack and the Beanstalk*. If Jack told the story, he would write,
I climbed and I climbed until I reached the top.
If you find the word 'I' or 'we' in a story, it is written in the 1st person.

Somebody watching the story would write,
Jack climbed and climbed until he reached the top.
If you find the word 'he', 'she' or 'they' in a story, it is written in the 3rd person.

Try this!
Read this passage and talk to a friend about what is wrong with it.

> One fine day, Jan and Pete went to the park. They ran all the way there. They were so excited. First they played on the swings, then we played football. We were just packing up when a dragon appeared! We were really scared.

Five finger check
When you write fables, ask yourself:

1. Have I thought of a moral?
2. How can I make it clear?
3. Am I going to use human or animal characters?
4. Am I going to use the pattern of three?
5. How will I plan?

Reflecting and reviewing

What have you learned about writing fables? Swap fables with another pair.

1. Read their fable. Is the moral clear?
2. Note down three things you know about writing fables.

Now complete your review sheet.

Unit 5
Performance poetry

Sensing My World

I like to watch
my cat stalk along the wall
then slip, slim as a wish,
beneath the gate.
I like to watch
the stars freckle the dark,
a thin moon's grin,
the city lights strung out
like fiery beads,
the belisha beacon blink
its orange eye,
the black taxis beetling
down back alleys,
the sudden rain making
goose pimples on the road.

Ears and eyes.
Nose and tongue –
with skin I prize
my world.

I like to listen to the sound
of the T.V. mumbling downstairs
as the night lengthens,
the scrunch of paper unwrapping,
a distant siren wobbling,
the chatter at the Saturday market stalls
and the deep warmth
of my mum's voice.

Ears and eyes.
Nose and tongue –
with skin I prize
my world.

I like the smell of
the salty sea wind in Cornwall,
bacon spitting in the frying pan,
chocolate mixed for a cake.

Ears and eyes.
Nose and tongue –
with skin I prize
my world.

I like the taste of
salty chips on a cold winter's night,
a bitter lemon,
the sweet bite of ice cream,
so cold that teeth ache,
the freshness of an apple slice.
I like the sudden fizz of cola
as it bursts in your mouth.

Ears and eyes.
Nose and tongue –
with skin I prize
my world.

Peter Bicot

Writing the poem

Using adjectives

What is an adjective?
An adjective is a word that describes a noun. It gives the reader more information about the noun. For example:
I ate a hot egg.
In this sentence the word *hot* adds extra description to the egg.

How are adjectives used?
When you are writing remember:

1. **Do not use too many adjectives, e.g.**
   The tall, large, handsome, cool, bright boy ran away.

2. **Do not use adjectives that tell the reader something they already know, e.g.**
   I swam in the wet water.

3. **Avoid using adjectives that all mean the same, e.g.**
   I looked at the large, big, enormous, colossal, walloping great giant.

4. **Select carefully to add something new or surprising, e.g.**
   The shy giant ran away.

5. **You do not always need an adjective, e.g.**
   The giant crushed the skyscraper.

   In this sentence you do not need to write, 'the *large* giant' because it is obvious from the rest of the sentence.

Quick write
Read the following sentences. Rewrite them including some adjectives. Decide which sounds better.

1. A dog chased a cat down the road.
2. The gnome hid under a mushroom.
3. The shark can be seen in the waters around the islands.

Preparing to write a poem
Most poets *brainstorm* ideas before writing. This means that they spend some time jotting down words and ideas. Some words they may never use in the poem, others they use and add to.

Here is an example of a brainstorm about special sounds:

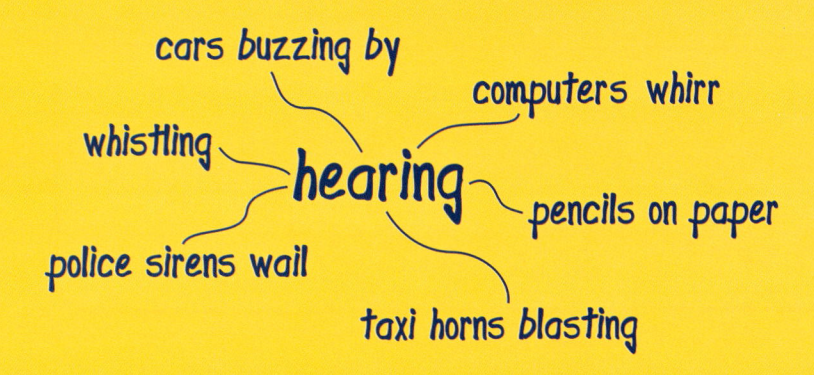

cars buzzing by
computers whirr
whistling
hearing
pencils on paper
police sirens wail
taxi horns blasting

Look at how the poet has taken some of these ideas, and added to them to create several lines of poetry:

I like the sound of
pencils busily scribbling words across my page,
the computer whirring as the screen blinks,
a police siren wailing in the night.

35

Polishing the poem

Tips for writing
- Jot down a quick list of ideas.
- Turn the best ideas into sentences.
- Select adjectives with care.

Try this!
Write your own senses poem. Use the class brainstorm and add your own ideas. Make a list of all your favourite sights, sounds, tastes, touches and smells.

Challenge
Write a verse that captures memories. For example:
I keep remembering
the sandy beach on holiday,
the day when our dog Hamlet died and
the sick feeling in my stomach.

Five finger check
When you read through the poem that you have written, ask yourself:

1. Does the poem sound effective?
2. Is each idea special?
3. Have I chosen my words and ideas carefully?
4. Do my adjectives add to the poem?
5. Does the poem make sense?

Writing a group chorus

To write a chorus you could use a simple counting pattern:

> 1, 2, 3, 4, 5 –
> feel my senses come alive.

Try ending on a different number:

> 1, 2, 3, 4 –
> my senses knock
> right at my door.

Or invent a simple rhyme:

> My ears and eyes,
> My tongue and my skin
> Let the world
> – enter in.

Try this!
Work with a partner to write a chorus for your group poem.

Reflecting and reviewing

What have you learned about performing a poem?
Talk to a partner. Think about:
- what worked well
- what could have been improved.

Now complete your review sheet.

Unit 6
Instructions

Find your way to the buried treasure. Think about what equipment you would need to take with you.

- sharks
- falling coconuts
- dangerous rocks
- boiling lava
- mangrove swamp
- cave
- crocodiles
- river with piranhas
- jungle
- snakes

North
West — East
South

volcano
treasure
vultures
slippery rocks
brambles
waterfall
poisonous bush
ravine
wild boars
tatty rope bridge
dangerous cliffs
aves with vampire bats
whirlpool

Planning instructions

What are instructions?
Instructions tell us how to do or make something. They may be *spoken* or *written*.

Spoken instructions
We use spoken instructions every day.

Don't forget to feed the cat!

Spoken instructions are not usually very exact because the listener already knows some information. For example, what the cat eats.

Written instructions
When we write instructions our reader can't ask us questions so we must write down exactly:
- what is needed
- what to do, in the right order.

Feeding a cat

What you need
- 1 tin cat food
- 1 spoon
- water
- 2 bowls

What you do
1. Open tin.
2. Spoon cat food into bowl.
3. Break up food.
4. Fill second bowl with fresh water.
5. Place both on the floor, away from sunlight.

Who is the audience?

When we use the word 'you' it shows that we want to speak or write directly to our audience. Sometimes we know the person we are writing for, sometimes we don't.

Instructions are sometimes written like this:
You turn right at the school.
The author is telling you what to do.

Writing directly to somebody is called writing in the 2nd person. Sometimes 'you' is missed out:
Turn right at the school.
But you still know the author is telling *you* what to do.

Making notes

Notes are a short and quick way to write.
We often use notes to:
- help us remember things
- write brief messages

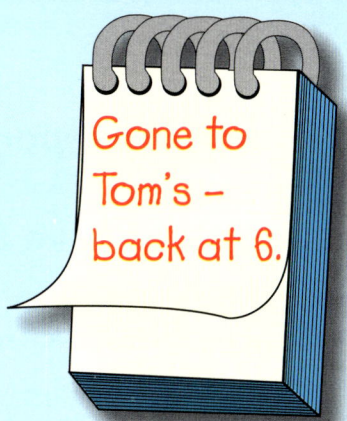

Take PE kit Tues.

Gone to Tom's – back at 6.

Notes can also help you to:
- plan your writing
- keep track of your ideas
- organise your ideas.

Tips for note making
- *leave out some words*
- *shorten words*
- *use lines and arrows to join ideas*
- *use numbers or bullet points for each new idea.*

Writing instructions

Try this!
Read these notes.

St M's sch
- 6 classes – 3 inf – 3 jnr
- 1 hall – PE, mtg, dining
- p'ground + climb fr n'ball ct
- field + f'ball p

Now read this report.

Our school is called St Mark's. There are six classrooms, three for the infants and three for the juniors. There is a hall which is used for PE, meetings and as a dining hall. There is a playground, where there is a climbing frame and a netball court. On the field next to the playground there is a football pitch.

Look at the notes and the report again.
Can you find:
- two abbreviations that have been turned into whole words?
- 15 words that have been added?

Organising notes

When you have made some notes it is a good idea to sort them out. If you group similar ideas together before you write it helps you make your writing clear for a reader.

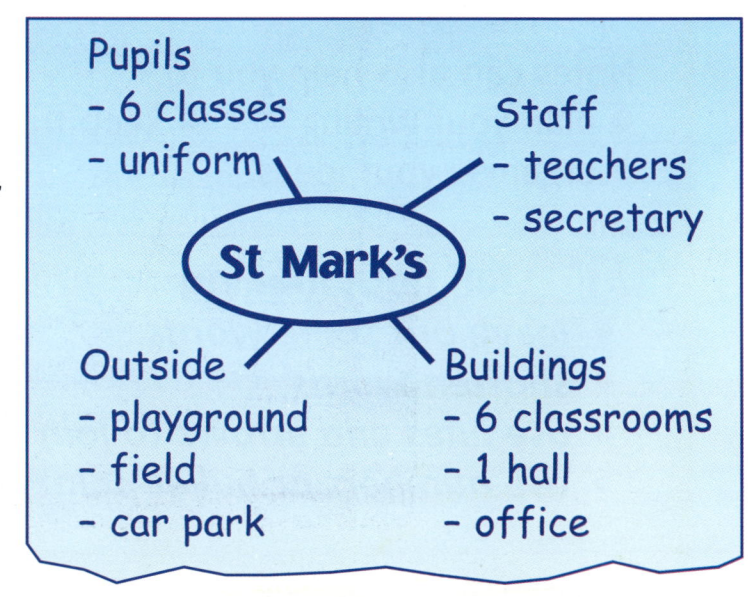

Pupils
- 6 classes
- uniform

Staff
- teachers
- secretary

St Mark's

Outside
- playground
- field
- car park

Buildings
- 6 classrooms
- 1 hall
- office

Challenge
How many words can you take out of this sentence? It must still make sense.
You have to walk carefully across the rickety old wooden bridge with the rotten ropes that stretches over the fast flowing river far below you.

Five finger check
When you write instructions, ask yourself:

1. What do I want my reader to do?
2. Have I given a list of what is needed?
3. Have I included all the steps in order?
4. Have I used different verbs near the beginning of each sentence?
5. Are the sentences short and clear?

Reflecting and reviewing

What have you learned about writing instructions?
1. Swap your map and directions with another pair.
2. Read their instructions. Can you follow them? Have they listed all the equipment needed?

Now complete your review sheet.

Unit 7
Extended stories

Think about an adventure story you can write that includes these characters and their galleon.

① Captain Slog

② Jack Knife

③ Molly Coddle

④ Jim Jam

Story ingredients
Stories have a set of ingredients, so writers often use a 'story recipe' to help them.

Story recipe

Ingredients
- Some tasty characters
- A delicious setting
- One or two chewy problems

Method
1. First think of some characters.
2. Next make your setting.
3. Then give the characters a problem or challenge.
4. After that, mix these together.
5. Then let the characters sort out the problem.
6. Finally add any extras you need to tell the tale.
7. Serve for a reader to enjoy.

Planning extended stories

Characters

What are they like?

Story writers help readers build up ideas about characters. They make characters in stories:

- do things
- think
- talk to other characters
- show their personalities.

Sometimes, writers give their characters names that give clues about what they are like.

Try this!

1. Read this passage.

   Justin Tyme was in a hurry. Hair unbrushed, jacket flapping and laces undone, he raced for the bus. As he puffed along, he wondered if Ms Crisp would believe his excuse this time.

2. Talk with a friend. What do you think this character is like? Why?

Challenge

What sort of a person do you think Ms Crisp could be? Write two or three sentences to describe Ms Crisp.

Planning stories

Planning stories helps writers organise their ideas. They follow a plan to:
- list ideas
- choose the best ideas
- sort ideas in the best order to tell the story.

> **Top Tip**
>
> **Making a plan before you write helps you write to the end.**

Pronouns

Pronouns are very useful words. They can be used to take the place of a noun. This means that we don't use the same noun over and over again which can make writing sound clumsy.

The chart below shows you how pronouns can:
- replace the names of people
- show who owns something.

Singular/Plural	Who/what	Owner
singular	I/me	mine
singular	you	yours
singular	he, she, it	his, hers, its
plural	we/us	ours
plural	you	yours
plural	they/them	theirs

Writing extended stories

Speech

Writers use speech marks to show the words their characters say. To help make speech clear, writers:
- use a new line for each new speaker
- use commas, question marks or exclamation marks to separate the speech from the speech verb
- use a capital letter to start a new speech.

Try this!
1. Look how the pictures and speech have been turned into writing.
2. How many differences can you spot?
3. How many punctuation marks are there?

A *I hope you can remember what I taught you yesterday.* — *Of course I can! Parrots never forget what they're told.*

B
'I hope you can remember what I taught you yesterday,' growled Black Jack.

'Of course I can!' squawked Patrick. 'Don't you know that parrots never forget what they're told?' he said as he furiously fluffed his feathers.

Time connectives

Writers have to let readers know that time passes in stories. They do this by using words that link events together in order, e.g. *soon, later, next, at last.*

Try this!
How many time connectives can you find in this passage?

Once, there were two ships. One day they set sail to search for treasure. They had soon left land far behind. After many days at sea they arrived on a lonely island. At last the crew stood on dry land.

Five finger check
When you are writing stories, ask yourself:

1. When and where does my story take place?
2. Who are the characters?
3. What are they like?
4. What is the problem?
5. How will it be solved?

Reflecting and reviewing

What have you learned about writing extended stories? Swap your story with a friend. Read each other's story, then discuss them. Think about the following points.

1. What are the characters like?
2. What is the problem they have to solve?
3. How did the story make you feel?

Now complete your review sheet.

Unit 8
Humorous poetry

When Jilly eats jelly,
Then Jilly is jolly.
But melons make Melanie
Most melancholy.

Colin West

Where Teachers Keep their Pets

Mrs Cox has a fox
Nesting in her curly locks.

Mr Spratt's tabby cat
Sleeps beneath his bobble hat.

Miss Cahoots has various newts
Swimming in her zip-up boots.

Mr Spry has Fred his fly
Eating food stains from his tie.

Mrs Groat shows off her stoat
Round the collar of her coat.

Mr Spare's got grizzly bears
Hiding in his big, wide flares.

And …

Mrs Vickers has a stick insect called 'Stickers'
… but no one's ever seen where she keeps it.

Paul Cookson

Creating alliteration

What is alliteration?
When a writer repeats the same sound close together in a line this is called *alliteration*. For example:
The bees buzz busily.

Writers use alliteration to draw the reader's attention to their writing. It can help to make a line memorable. Adverts often use alliteration, for example:
Try some tempting Toffee Treats today!

What is a tongue twister?
A tongue twister is a brief rhyme or saying that has lots of alliteration. So the words sound very similar and are difficult to say without getting muddled. How quickly can you say these tongue twisters without getting the words muddled?

Red lorry, yellow lorry.

She sells sea shells on the sea shore.

How much wood could a woodchuck chuck if a woodchuck could chuck wood?

Quick write
Make a tongue twister. Read these sentences aloud, filling in the gaps with a word that starts with the same sound.

1. S... Simon sat sewing some s... socks.
2. T... Tina tried to tell a t... tale.
3. B... Bernard broke a b... buckle by b... .

Tips for writing an alliterative alphabet poem
1. Think of the name of a character for each letter of the alphabet, e.g. Bill.
2. Find an adjective for each name, e.g. Brave Bill.
3. Now think of a verb, e.g. Brave Bill bought . . .
4. Extend the sentence as far as you can, trying to use as many of the same sounds as possible, e.g.
   Brave Bill bought a beautiful, blue balloon but it burst.
5. If you get stuck, miss the line out. You can always go back to it. Using a dictionary may help.

Tips for writing rhyming couplets
1. For your poem think about the name of a creature that can end the first line. Choose one that gives you plenty of rhymes, e.g. croc.
2. Now invent the name of a teacher that rhymes with the creature, e.g. Mrs Brock.
3. Now write the first line, e.g.
   Mrs Brock has got a one-eyed croc.
4. Now think about possible words that rhyme with 'croc', e.g.
   block, dock, frock, mock, knock, stock, rock.
5. Invent a second line, e.g.

Mrs Brock has got a one-eyed croc,
That gave the postman a mighty shock.

Polishing the poem

Try this!

Read your poem through and listen to how it sounds.

1. Work on any lines that seem too long or too short.
2. Keep changing the words until both lines in the couplets have the same rhythm or beat.
3. Are there any lines that do not work well or do not make sense?
4. Are there any words that might be improved?

Challenge

Read the sentences carefully. Can you complete the rhymes?

1. You make me want to ride on a goat.
   You make me want to . . .

2. You make me want to go for a run.
   You make me want to . . .

3. You make me want to buy a parrot.
   You make me want to . . .

Five finger check
When you read through the poem that you have written, ask yourself:

1. Does the poem sound effective?
2. Are some of the ideas amusing?
3. Have I chosen my words and ideas carefully?
4. Are the lines rhythmic?
5. Does the poem flow well when I read it aloud?

Reflecting and reviewing

What have you learned about writing humorous poetry? Talk to a partner.

Think about:
1. Which was the most memorable couplet?
2. What was good about your performance?
3. How could you have improved it?

Now complete your review sheet.

Unit 9
Recounts

Think about what is happening in the photograph.

Challenge
Write a caption that describes what is happening in the photograph.

Successful School Fête

Last Saturday, 27th June, Castle Hill Primary School held a summer fête. The event took place on the sports field, behind the school. The fête was opened at 2 o'clock by Eastlife. This well-known boy band are all ex-pupils of Castle Hill Primary School.

The afternoon's events started with a display by the school juggling team. Then at 3 o'clock, Castle Hill's steel band entertained the crowds. Next the competition for the cuddliest pet took place. At 4 o'clock, Year 6 pupils served cream teas in the tea tent.

Finally, at about 5 o'clock, Mrs Pipps, the headteacher, announced the winners of the raffle and thanked everybody for coming. She said, 'This has been a wonderful afternoon. Everybody has had a good time and we've raised enough money to buy a new computer. We'll certainly do this again next year.'

Planning a recount

What is a recount?
A recount gives information about something that has happened, for example, a visit, an accident, a sports event. Recounts tell:
- when the event happened
- what happened
- why it happened.
- who was involved
- where it happened

Sometimes recounts end by letting the readers know how people felt about the event.

Recounts can be found in letters, e-mails, diaries, newspapers and newsletters.

Recounts can also be spoken. When you are telling your friends about something that has happened, you are giving a recount.

> **Remember!** *Recounts are always in the past tense. They can be written in the 1st person, e.g. I went... or the 3rd person, e.g. He went...*

Point of view
Our point of view is:
- how we feel about something
- what we think about something.

So, if we recount an event that we have been part of, our point of view makes a difference to how we tell it.

Some things that add to our point of view are:
- what we know about this sort of event
- what we **see**
- whether we know anybody in the event.

Try this!

Read these two recounts about the same event.

1. What's the same and what's different?

A **The Dads' Race**

Last week it was Sports Day at Dan's school. I had agreed to run in the Dads' race (again!). Last year I was beaten by Andy's dad and I did not want that to happen again.

We lined up on the starting line. My heart was banging away, I was really nervous. We were off. I ran as fast as I could, but I could hear Andy's dad coming up behind me.

Then just as he was about to overtake me, I heard Dan shout, 'Come on Dad!' I put in more effort, and to my amazement, I won!

B **The Dads' Race**

It was our school Sports Day last week. My dad was entered in the Dads' race. He's really great. Last year Andy's dad won, but only because my dad let him.

I watched Dad jogging around on the starting line in his new trainers. He looked calm and confident. I knew he'd win. They were off! Dad sped up the track but Andy's dad was close behind him.

'Come on Dad!' I yelled. As if by magic, he sped on and, as I expected, he won!

2. Can you work out who is giving each recount and why they are different?

Writing a recount

Informal and formal recounts
When writers know who will read their recounts, they often write in a chatty or *informal* way, as if they were talking to each other, for example A.
When writers don't know their readers they write in a more *formal* way, for example B.

A

Dear Jack

Guess what? Last Saturday Jo and I went to see Toy Story 4 down at the new cinema. It was great. You must go and see it.

Love

Bianca

B

On Saturday 4th October Bianca Smythe, together with her best friend Jo, went to see Toy Story 4 at the new Triangle Cinema in Portsdown. After the show Bianca Smythe said it was the best film she had ever seen.

Try this!
Reread the two recounts above.
1. What is the same?
2. What is different?

Time

When we write recounts we need to make the order of events clear. So we use time words to connect events. Time connectives include words and phrases like: *first, next, later, soon, in the end.*

Sometimes we use dates and times to show *exactly* when things happened. For example:

The raffle was held on Wednesday 8th February at 10 o'clock in the morning.

Five finger check

When you write recounts, ask yourself:

1. Who is it about?
2. When did it happen?
3. Where did it happen?
4. What happened, in order?
5. Who is telling the recount?

Reflecting and reviewing

What have you learned about writing recounts? Swap your recount with a friend. Read it and think about the following points.

1. Is it clear who is telling the recount?
2. Do you think other improvements could be made?

Now complete your review sheet.

Word classes

English words can be divided into eight groups. These groups are called word classes. The class names are:

*nouns   adjectives   verbs   adverbs
pronouns   prepositions   conjunctions   determiners.*

Each word class has its own job to do in a sentence.

Nouns

This is a large class. It contains all the words that name something or somebody.
There are different kinds of nouns:

Proper nouns
These are the names of particular people, places or things. These nouns always start with a capital letter e.g. *Joe, April, Leeds*.

Common nouns
These are the names of ordinary things e.g. *sister, dog, shop*.

Abstract nouns
These are the names of feelings and other things that can be thought about but not seen e.g. *love, truth*.

Collective nouns
The names of groups of things e.g. *crowd, flock, herd*.

Some nouns can be singular or plural e.g. *dog/dogs, table/tables*. These are called **countable nouns** because you can count more than one. Other nouns, like *money, butter* and *cotton* do not change in the plural. These are called **mass nouns**.

Adjectives

This is another large class of words. Adjectives are words that are used to describe a noun or pronoun. They can come before or after a noun e.g. *the **tall** man* or *the man was **tall***.
Adjectives can make comparisons e.g. *the **tall** man, the **taller** man, the **tallest** man*.

Pronouns

Pronouns are words that can be used in place of a noun.
You can write:
The boy ran away. The boy ran too fast and fell over.
You can use a pronoun instead: *The boy ran away. **He** ran too fast and fell over.*
Examples of pronouns are: *he, she, it, them, they, his, my, yourself, who, what.*

Prepositions

Prepositions link two nouns or pronouns. They tell us about:
- time e.g. *They left **at** lunchtime.*
- position e.g. *The boy climbed **over** the chair.*
- direction e.g. *She jumped **towards** the ledge.*

Verbs

This is an important word class because every sentence must have a verb in it. Verbs tell us two things:
- what happens,
  e.g. *Dan **kicked** the ball.*
  *The builder **lifts** the bricks.*
- when things happen. This is called the *tense*.

*Present tense: Dan **kicks** the ball.*
the action is happening now.
*Past tense: Dan **kicked** the ball.*
the action has already happened.
*Future tense: Dan **will kick** the ball.*
the action is going to happen.

Conjunctions

Conjunctions connect parts of a sentence. They can do different jobs.

They can be used to join two simple sentences using *and, or, but,* or *so.*
e.g. *Fred went to the shops **and** he bought some stickers.*

They can also be used to join a clause or phrase to a sentence:
e.g. *Fred went to the shop **although** he did not have any money.*
*Fred went to the shop **because** he wanted some stickers.*
*Fred went to the shop **when** the rain stopped.*

Adverbs

Adverbs give more information about verbs and sometimes about adjectives.

Many adverbs end in *'ly'*
They often answer these questions:
how? *quietly,*
how much? *very,*
where? *outside,*
when? *soon,*
how often? *never.*

Many words can be included in more than one class depending on their job in a sentence
e.g. *Hit* can be a noun:
*The **hit** of the week was 'Go Now' by the group Girlzone.*
or a verb:
*She **hit** the ball into the net.*
Blue *can be a noun: **Blue** is a colour,*
an adjective: *The bottle is **blue***
or an adverb: *She was feeling **blue**.*

Determiners

These are some of the most common words in the English language
e.g. *a, an, the.*
Determiners refer to a noun
e.g. *the dog, that table, a girl.*

63

Glossary

Look here to find or check the meaning of some of the words used in the Writer's Handbook or that are used by writers.

audience a word used to describe anybody who watches a film or play, listens to speakers or singers or reads something; when we write, the audience is the people who read our writing

characters people or animals in a story or play

formal writing a polite style of writing, usually used when a writer and reader don't know each other

informal writing a chatty, friendly style of writing, usually used when the writer and reader know each other

narrator the person who tells the story

paragraph a group of sentences in a piece of writing; writers use paragraphs to collect similar ideas together

point of view how somebody describes an event, or thinks about something

setting where and when a story takes place; the setting of a story is like the scenery in a play or film

speech words spoken by characters

technical vocabulary words used in non-fiction texts that relate to a particular subject, e.g. *rain* is a technical word when you write about the weather